D

BA

ON FOOT

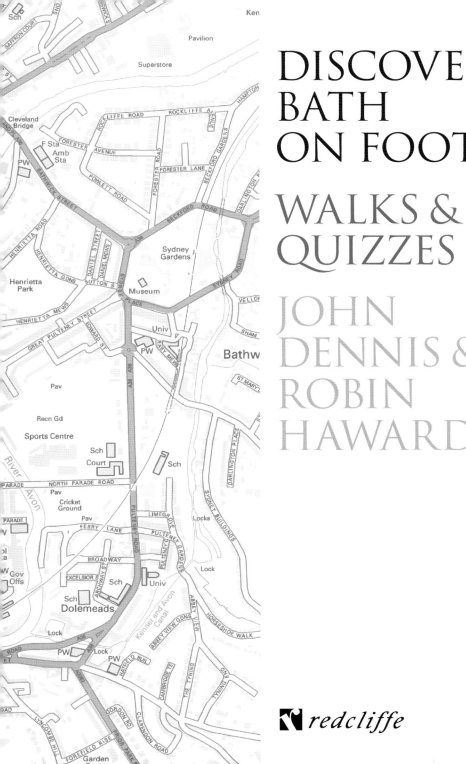

DISCOVER
BATH
ON FOOT

WALKS &
QUIZZES

JOHN
DENNIS &
ROBIN
HAWARD

ℕ *redcliffe*

First published in 2010 by Redcliffe Press Ltd.,
81G Pembroke Road, Bristol BS8 3EA
www.redcliffepress.co.uk | info@redcliffepress.co.uk

Map created by Maps International.co.uk Based upon Ordnance Survey digital map data
© Crown Copyright 2010 Licence Number 43368U. All rights reserved.

ISBN 978-1-906593-57-5
British Library Cataloguing-in-Publication Data
A catalogue record for this book is available from the British Library

Design and typesetting by E&P Design, Bath
Printed by Hobbs The Printers Ltd, Totton, Hampshire

CONTENTS

INTRODUCTION

Bath has never been short of good guide books to take you through the Roman and Georgian treasures of the city. This book aims to take you beyond that to look at different aspects of this marvellous place.

Our thanks must go again to our band of checkers for their suggestions and constructive comments. Angela Haward has been of particular help together with Mariasol Dennis, Nick Haward, Nick Parsons, Sarah Scott and Paula Whiting. A special thank-you to our photographer Bob Bell, whose enthusiasm and eye for detail have made the photographs such an integral part of the book.

Finally we would like to thank our publishers, Redcliffe Press, especially John, Angela and Clara Sansom.

We hope you enjoy discovering Bath on foot.

A few words from the Right Reverend Peter Price, Bishop of Bath and Wells

'Bath is a beautiful City and I am delighted that these walks begin and end at the wonderful West door of the Abbey. I hope that visitors and residents alike will have time to go in and admire the Abbey and appreciate its atmosphere of quiet contemplation. I believe that the best way to get to know a place is to 'walk it' and users of this book will discover the less well-known features of Bath, as well as the more famous.

'Robin Haward is an old friend and colleague whose passion for seeing places on foot gives him a particular perspective. I do hope you enjoy discovering the Bath that Robin and John have walked so faithfully.'

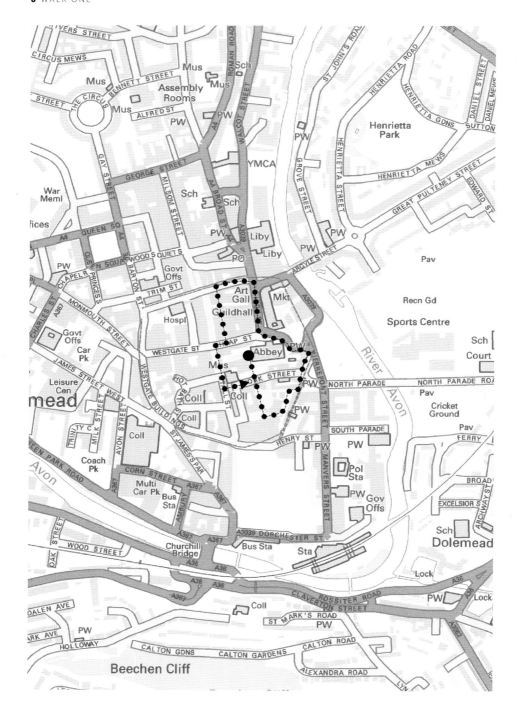

WALK 1
ROUND THE ABBEY

1

Stand with your back to the main Abbey door at the West End and turn left. Walk past the small door and round the corner of the buttress.

▶ *Who was R.G. Askew?*

2

Walk down by the wall to York Street, cross and enter Abbey Street.

▶ *What can you find on the wall of Elton House?*

3

Continue a couple of yards and on your right:

▶ *What is The Crystal Palace?*

4

You are in Abbey Green. Admire the superb plane tree in the centre. Continue towards the arch and stand under it. You are in Abbey Gate.

▶ *What is the date of the map displayed under the arch?*

5

Turn left at the bottom, by the door of Marks and Spencer, and walk up the slope in front of you, turning left into North Parade Buildings.

▶ *Opposite the path leading in from your left, what name can you see on the buildings?*

6

Continue until the end and look at the plaque on your right.

▶ *When did John Palmer die?*

Study Sally Lunn's in front of you.

▶ *Why did she come to Bath?*

7

Turn right into North Parade and, near the end on the right, look at Victoria House.

▶ *What is the plaque at first-floor level?*

Now turn to your left and walk towards York Street. Cross over York Street and walk straight ahead into the Orange Grove.

WORLD HERITAGE SITE

This is an important status for the City of Bath and it will be no surprise to you, having looked around, that Bath acquired World Heritage Site status in 1987. The status is conferred by the United Nations Educational, Scientific and Cultural Organisation (UNESCO). It is all to do with conserving mankind's cultural and natural heritage. By signing up to the World Heritage Convention our government has shown that it is committed to those aims.

In 2010 there were 890 World Heritage Sites throughout the world, with 28 of those being in the UK. So Bath is part of a larger family which includes the Pyramids, Victoria Falls and the Great Barrier Reef. Being a World Heritage Site has enormous advantages for Bath; but as well as world-wide recognition there are obligations to do with the way visitors are received and the way the site is managed, protected and conserved. It is a good example of the ways that local authorities work with government.

Turn left and walk towards the Abbey's east window. Study the sign under the window.

▶ *Who gave the sign?*

Move to your right slightly and look at the plaque on the buttress.

▶ *What happened on Whit Sunday 973?*

Continue round the Abbey and cross at the light-controlled crossing. Continue up High Street for a few yards and then look left.

▶ *When was The Old Bank established?*

North Parade Buildings

Sally Lunn's

Continue up past Guildhall and search for information carved in the stone.

▶ *When were Bath City Markets given the Royal Charter?*

Cross at the end of High Street to Upper Borough Walls and find the plaque on the building near the junction.

▶ *Which gate to the city was sited here?*

Walk up Upper Borough Walls and then turn left into Union Passage.

▶ *What is the name on the building at the junction with Northumberland Place?*

BEAU NASH

Bath was a pretty wild place when Richard Nash first arrived – a hotbed of gambling and unruly behaviour. It was the eighteenth-century equivalent of Las Vegas with a bit of Dodge City thrown in. Nash became its Master of Ceremonies because his predecessor had just been killed in a duel!

Richard Nash came originally from Swansea and his early life was undistinguished, to say the least. He never finished his studies at Oxford University and then had unsuccessful stints in the army and as a lawyer. His time in the Guards Division in London gave him the opportunity to develop his 'contacts' and he then set about his true vocation – gambling!

The job of Master of Ceremonies was to arrange the social life of the city – balls, concerts, card parties, etc – and ensure their smooth running. He took to the job easily and soon assumed the title 'King of Bath'. His nickname 'Beau' came about as a result of his elegant (and sometimes outlandish) dress style.

Beau Nash's 'Rules of Bath' make good reading. You will find them on tea-towels etc. at various shops in the city.

Figures round the Guildhall

Continue straight down Union Passage to emerge into Cheap Street. Turn right and walk up to the crossroads with Stall Street, Westgate Street and Union Street. Study the building on the junction of Union Street and Westgate Street.

▶ *How many 'human' heads are there on this building?*
▶ *What is the date on the building?*

Turn left down Stall Street and look closely at the first colonnade on your left.

▶ *How many columns can you see? Include them even if they are visible but not completely free-standing.*

Study the entrance to the pump room on this street.

▶ *When was the City of Bath entered on the World Heritage List?*
▶ *What words can you see carved in the stone above the door?*

Continue and turn left into York Street. Walk for about 20 yards until you come to a stone plaque on your left.

▶ *In what were the baths of Aquae Sulis unequalled?*

Continue along York Street and study the end of the last building on the right at the junction with Abbey Street.

▶ *How many arches appear to have been filled in?*

Turn left and you are back at the Abbey ●

The plane tree on Abbey Green

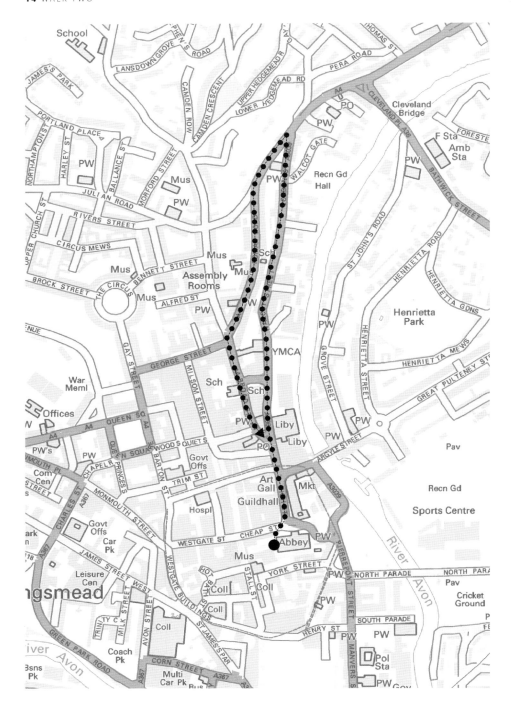

WALK 2
WALCOT

Start with your back to the main Abbey door and turn right, walking round the corner of the Abbey. Cross at the crossing to High Street. Walk up High Street past the Guildhall and continue straight up Northgate. Then take a rightish fork at the Podium and wander up Walcot Street. Continue past the Bath Hilton and then pause opposite the YMCA. Turn and look across to the distant hill.

▶ *What can you see on the hillside (difficult when the trees are in leaf)? It is distant and near the skyline.*

Continue for a few yards and stop at number 62.

▶ *What has number 62 been in the past?*

Walk up Walcot Street until you reach Beehive Yard. Enter the yard and study the old Tramshed.

▶ *How many windows are there at first-floor level above, and on the same wall as, the clock?*

Leave Beehive Yard and continue up Walcot Street. Opposite a long flight of steps cross to the drinking fountain.

▶ *Supply the missing word: '…springing up into _____ life.'*
▶ *What does it seem you need to do to get your rest?*

Turn and look back across the road.

▶ *What date can you find on a building?*

Walk up Walcot Street for a few yards until you reach St Michael's Church House and look above the door.

▶ *Who is the figure in stone?*

Keep walking up the street and cross Old Orchard.

▶ *It was established in 1798 but when was the porch erected?*

Walk a few yards.

▶ *Who lived 'above' the office?*

Continue up the street and then turn right down Chatham Row and find number 12.

▶ *What award did the row achieve?*

Return to Walcot Street and study the walls around the wonderful pub, The Bell.

▶ *Where were Hopleaf Ales brewed?*

Walk on up the street passing The Bell and turn and study numbers 124 and 126 opposite.

▶ *What is odd about the first-floor windows?*

Cross the road and continue up the street, turning right into Walcot Gate. Look right at the little chapel. If the gates are open it is worth wandering in.

▶ *When was the chapel erected?*

Drinking fountain, Walcot Street

A Penfold hexagonal post box

THE PULTENEY RADIAL GATE

This looks to be an impressive piece of engineering – and it is!

If you look at it carefully you can easily work out how it functions. But what is its purpose? Why is it here next to the weir?

It was built in 1972 as part of a scheme to protect Bath from flooding. If you have seen the river Avon after a lot of rain you'll see the need: the weir disappears under water when the river is very high. The radial gate was put in to allow a lot of water to pass through and downstream when the river was high. It also allows control over the amount of water left upstream when water levels are low. It looks as though the system is coping without it now… so it's a bit of a relic, albeit an interesting one.

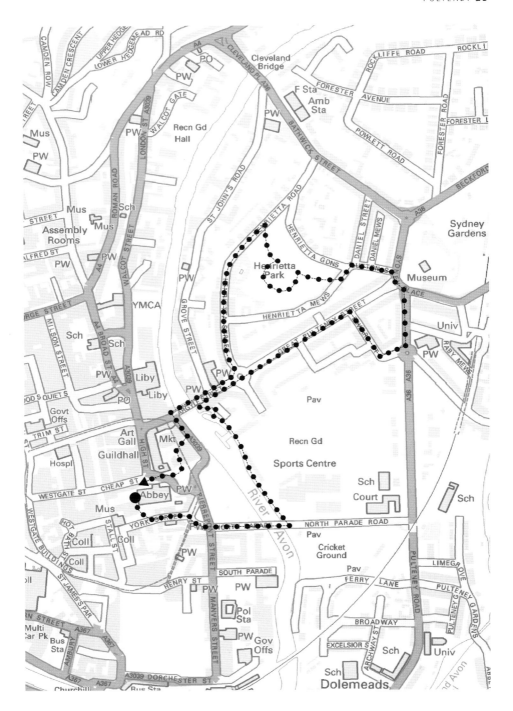

The weir and Pulteney Bridge

Study the Pulteney Radial Gate.

▶ *When was the weir opened?*

Walk along to a display board.

▶ *Who was King Lear's father?*

Continue along the path bearing left and near the river. Climb the steps in the corner by a café. At the top of the steps continue along Argyle Street. When you reach the junction with Grove Street, look across the road.

▶ *What does the picture on the wall tell us about the building on the corner?*

Continue along the street to Laura Place and bear right. At the entrance to Johnstone Street look at number 15.

▶ *Who lived here in 1802?*

Continue walking along what is now Great Pulteney Street.

▶ *Who lived at number 76?*
▶ *What is outside The Windsor?*

Carry on along the street to number 55.

▶ *Who stayed here in 1846?*

WALK 3
PULTENEY

With the main door of the Abbey behind you, turn left and walk diagonally across the square. Turn left and continue down York Street.

▶ *Look on your right. Who lived next door to the Quakers?*

At the end of the street bear right along North Parade and then cross straight over at the lights to the far side of Pierrepont Street. Continue down Pierrepont Street until you find a plaque to James Quin.

▶ *When did James Quin die?*

Continue back towards the lights and look for the answers to these questions:

▶ *When was the Earl of Chesterfield born?*
▶ *Which famous Admiral lived a few yards nearer to the junction?*

Turn right at the lights and continue along North Parade. After a few yards:

▶ *Who lived at the Parade Park?*

Walk to house number 11.

▶ *Who stayed here in 1771?*
▶ *What can you find on the corner of Duke Street and North Parade?*

Continue along North Parade and when you reach the bridge very carefully cross the road.

▶ *Who built the bridge – and when?*

Cross over the bridge and when you reach the small tower descend the staircase inside to the river bank. As you emerge turn right and walk along towards the weir. Look across at the excellent view of the Abbey.

▶ *How many church spires can you see?*

Continue along the path until you reach a flight of steps.

▶ *When did the first cargo using the River Avon Navigation arrive here?*
▶ *Who has a ticket office here?*

Hay Hill

Walk on and when you reach the Saracen's Head, look across to the inn.

▶ *What date can you find on the inn?*

Carry on down to the corner beyond the post office and enter the porch.

▶ *What did Ralph Allen reorganise and perfect?*
▶ *What did John Palmer develop?*

Retrace your steps from the beginning of the walk and you're back at the Abbey ●

Retrace your steps until you are opposite the break in the railings outside The Star Inn. Look across the road.

▶ *What is the term used instead of 'pub'?*

Very carefully cross the road and turn left, walking along the raised pavement. Pause outside number 20 and look back.

▶ *What is the connection with education?*

Walk along the raised pavement until you reach the Countess of Huntingdon's Chapel.

▶ *When was the chapel founded?*
▶ *What was her Christian name?*

Continue until the junction with Hay Hill.

▶ *Years ago, what would you have found here?*

Keep going along the raised pavement, passing Hay Hill Baptist Church and at the end turn left, crossing at the lights – be very careful and watch out for turning traffic. You will arrive at the top of Broad Street. Continue down the right-hand side of Broad Street until you come to King Edward's School on your right.

▶ *When was the school founded?*
▶ *Who designed the building we see now?*

15

Continue along the pavement past
St Swithin's Church.

▶ *What happened to the tower in 1790?*

16

Walk on a few yards and study the
beginning of the long terrace.

▶ *What is the first name you find in
the stone?*

17

Continue to house number 33.

▶ *Who lived here?*

18

Carry on along the pavement to number 27.

▶ *What do you think all the carved letters
mean? Would it help if we told you that
'P' meant Parish?*

JOHN PALMER

John Palmer spent a lot of time travelling
in coaches as a young man. He was the
manager of the theatre (later to become
the Theatre Royal) in Orchard Street and
later took on the Bristol theatre, also given
a Royal Patent. He used the same company
of actors in each theatre, and transported
them back and forth by coach – a rehearsal
in Bristol during the day, then a performance
in Bath that evening. He also had to travel
to London regularly to interview new
actors and see new plays. He knew plenty
about the state of the country's roads and
the inefficiency of the postal service.

Mail at this time was delivered by post
riders, horse riders travelling unaccompanied
and unarmed. Pace was slow and highway
robbery common-place. The journey from
Bath to London took at least 36 hours.

Palmer's plan was to adapt the stage-
coaches of the time to carry the mail. It
would be kept in a strongbox in the coach
with an armed guard on duty at all times.

The Post Office in London was not
impressed with the idea. It saw no reason
to change the present system and, besides,
it would be much more expensive.

Eventually Palmer persuaded William Pitt,
the Chancellor of the Exchequer, to allow
him a trial run.

On 2 August, 1784 a coach left the Rummer
in Bristol at 4 p.m., called at The Three Tuns
in Bath at 5.30 p.m., and then on to The
Swan With Two Necks, Lad Lane in London,
arriving at 8 a.m. the following morning.
Sixteen hours against thirty six! The coach
came back to Bristol that night in the same
time. Within a month there were services
planned from London to Norwich,
Nottingham, Liverpool and Manchester.

For more than 50 years John Palmer's
mail coaches ruled supreme.

Then came the railway.

St Swithin's Church

PARISH BOUNDARIES

You could study parish boundaries in England for weeks – and still not get to the bottom of the subject. Clearly in the past they were of great importance. The parish was responsible for the people who lived within it and this would include things like poor relief and even street lighting. Residents within the parish would pay rates to the parish for the provision of these services, so you can see that it was important to know where the boundaries were. The boundaries would be checked each year by officers who walked the bounds and checked that all the parish boundary markers were in place. They were often given numbers so that the presence of each sign could be checked.

13

Return to Walcot Street and walk to the top and then:

▶ *What has Walcot Street turned into?*

14

Cross carefully, drop down a few feet and walk up the flight of steps by St Swithin's Church. Continue along the pavement and look through the railings at the plaques.

▶ *What was the Christian name of Jane Austen's mother?*
▶ *When did George Austen die?*
▶ *Who wrote* **The Wanderer?**

The bell at The Bell

Turn right into Edward Street and when you reach number 12 cross the road.

▶ *Who lived at number 10?*

At the end of the street turn left into Vane Street. At the end of Vane Street turn left into Darlington Street. Walk to the end, cross Great Pulteney Street (watch out for the high kerb) and enter Sutton Street.

▶ *How many filled-in windows can you see?*

Continue down Sutton Street.

▶ *What is the name of the pub at the junction with Daniel Street?*
▶ *Roughly when was it established?*

Enter Henrietta Gardens in front of you and, keeping to the paths, walk straight across until you reach the circular path. Then walk left, clockwise, until you reach the railings around the Garden of Remembrance. Bear left to find a stone tablet in the laurel bushes.

▶ *Who presented this park to the city of Bath?*

Fred Weatherly's window

Continue up the path and leave the park, turning left into Henrietta Road.

▶ *What sign can you find above numbers 22 and 23?*
▶ *And where else?*

Walk left again to find a plaque on the railings.

▶ *In whose honour is the Garden of Remembrance dedicated?*

Walk along to the junction with Henrietta Mews.

▶ *What may you NOT do under the arch?*

Continue up Henrietta Street to the top and then turn right into Argyle Street.

▶ *How many sides has the Victorian post box?*
▶ *Who was the architect of Laura Place?*

Look across the street.

▶ *Which animals can you see above the chemist?*

Walk back over Pulteney Bridge and turn immediately left into Grand Parade. At once look for a plaque.

▶ *Who was the architect of Pulteney Bridge?*
▶ *When was it built?*

Safely cross the road and turn right just beyond the market entrance by the Rummer Pub. Walk up the alley and with care enter the car park.

▶ *How long has the Guildhall market served Bath?*

Walk through the car park and exit through the arch and, turning right, you are back at the Abbey ●

A glimpse of Ralph Allen's house

SEDAN CHAIRS

The Sedan Chair gets its name from the little town in eastern France, close to the Belgian border, where it made its first appearance. This was in the 1580s, but it was 50 years later that the chairs became established, when Sir Saunders Dunscombe obtained a licence to hire them out (originally in London).

The public sedan was a single-seated upholstered chair, surrounded on three sides by a frame with windows and a roof that could be raised to allow you to climb in more easily. It was mounted on long springy poles to be carried by two chairmen, one at the front, one at the back, and reports claimed that it was indeed a bouncy ride!

Visitors to Bath found them particularly convenient and attractive as a means of transport. These people would have come here either for the social life or for health reasons, and it was so much better to travel the less-than-perfect streets, all dressed-up, without being rained on or splattered with mud. And the special feature of the sedan chair was that you were not only transported door-to-door, but indoors too, in fact into the very room in which you were staying! This was particularly attractive to those invalids who had come to Bath to take the waters.

You picked up your sedan in the street (you can see the only sedan chair houses left in the country at Queen's Parade Place), and could be hired at all hours of the day or night.

The fashion of travelling by sedan finally came to an end with the invention of another form of transport; John Heath, a Bathonian, invented the Bath Chair.

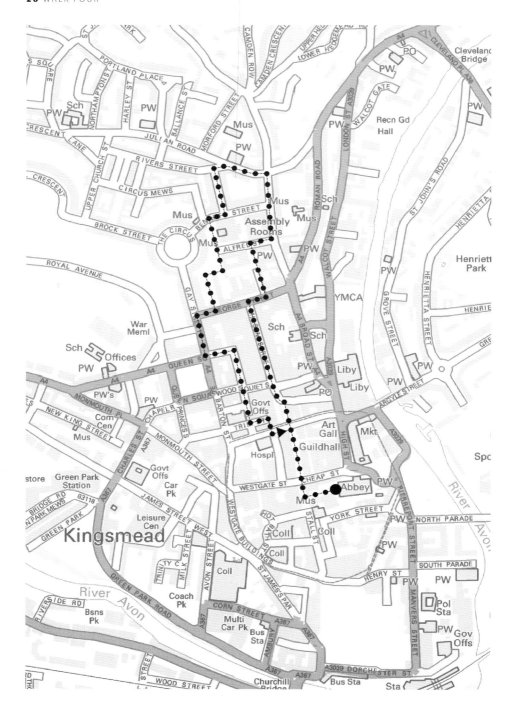

WALK 4
ASSEMBLY ROOMS

Stand with your back to the Abbey door and walk straight across to the colonnade. Go through and turn right. Continue straight up to Milsom Street and walk up to the top. At the top cross straight over at the lights and enter Bartlett Street.

▶ *Which Saint has a terrace here?*

Continue to the top and turn right into Alfred Street. Find number 2.

▶ *Who lived here in 1783?*

At the end of the street cross and continue up the hill.

▶ *Look at Belmont opposite. What's interesting about the door of number 12?*

Continue up the hill.

▶ *What is distinctive about number 18?*
▶ *What is strange about the left of number 20?*

Turn left into Julian Road.

▶ *What French connection can you immediately find?*

Find Christchurch on your right.

▶ *When was it consecrated?*
▶ *What is the date on number 11, the building round the back?*

Turn left opposite Christchurch and walk down River's Street a little way.

▶ *What faces down Russell Street?*

Turn left and continue down Russell Street.

▶ *What can you find on the wall outside number 13?*
▶ *What is odd about the windows of the house at the bottom of Russell Street?*
▶ *Which King has a pillar box at the bottom of the street?*

The entrance to the Assembly Rooms

Cross to the Assembly Rooms and pause at the entrance. If you have time, and they are open, you could go in. In the entrance:

▶ *When were they opened?*
▶ *Who designed them?*
▶ *Where would you play cards?*

Walk a few yards further to the end of Alfred Street.

▶ *Who is above the door of number 14?*
▶ *What else does it have besides torch snuffers?*

Walk down the alleyway, St Andrew's Terrace. Turn right at the bottom and then left into Miles's Buildings.

▶ *What has number 6 got that the others have not?*
▶ *What is the name of the pub at the bottom?*
▶ *How much would it cost you to cycle on the pavement here?*

BATH'S MEDIEVAL CITY WALLS

These are fun to find and to go and look at. There are two places to go: Upper Borough Walls and East Gate behind the Guildhall. There are other sections and fragments to be found. The medieval walls were impressive. At the base they were about three metres wide and they would have reached something like six metres in height.

Medieval cities needed to protect their citizens and the activities which went on inside them. Clearly these walls would have restricted the comings and goings of travellers and traders so it would be possible to impose tolls and taxes.

Gradually, as Bath grew, the medieval walls became more and more of a nuisance. The gates were too narrow and the walls were in the way of the massive development of the mid-eighteenth century – so most were demolished to make way for the new streets. Admire the section of the wall in Upper Borough Walls opposite the hospital and think: security, safety and control.

Christchurch

Miles's Buildings

Descend the steps and cross the road, being very careful. Turn right and walk along George Street to the junction with Gay Street and then turn left down Gay Street. Look across the road to Queen's Parade Place.

▶ *How many blocked-in windows are there?*

Continue down Gay Street.

▶ *What do you find at number 40?*
▶ *What do you find above the door of 41?*

Look through the window at the right of the door.

▶ *What colour are the tiles?*

Turn left into Old King Street.

▶ *When did John Wood junior die?*

At the end of the street turn right down John Street. On your right. Until very recently there was, on the walls of the old Bonhams Auction House, artwork depicting the Magna Carta. This has been removed. Shame!

Continue to the bottom of the street.

▶ *What is the profession of Messrs Paxton and Whitfield?*

WINDOW TAX

If you were to stand in Beauford Square by the original entrance to the Theatre Royal (the present entrance came much later after the theatre was damaged by fire) you would see, in the houses opposite, a series of bricked-up windows. This came about as a result of the Window Tax.

Governments have always been looking for ways to get money from us through taxes. Before the Window Tax there was the Hearth Tax. This meant the householder was taxed according to how many fireplaces he had, but, as you can well imagine, the householder wasn't keen to let the taxman come in and count, so the government resorted to counting the number of chimneys on the roof. This sounded a good idea, but the ingenious builders would position the fireplaces at the corner of the room, next to the centre wall, and the one in the next room similarly next to the centre wall. Two hearths, one chimney. And if the builders put two more directly above the first two, one chimney would service four!

Time for a re-think, so in 1696 the Window Tax was introduced, and any house with more than six windows was taxed. Houses with seven to nine windows meant the tax was two shillings, ten to twenty windows, four shillings. Hence the bricking up of the windows. The tax lasted until 1851.

Cross carefully and enter Queen Street.

▶ *What can you find on the wall opposite the Raven?*

Continue through the arch and turn left into Trim Street.

▶ *Which famous general lived at number 5?*

Follow the road round to the right and at the end turn right for a few yards.

▶ *What is special about the wall?*

Retrace your steps and continue a few yards.

▶ *When was the Royal Mineral Water Hospital founded?*

Turn right into Union Street and then shortly left into Northumberland Place. Turn right and continue to the junction at the bottom.

▶ *What is the name of the street you have just walked down?*

Cross Cheap Street, go through the alley and you are back at the Abbey ●

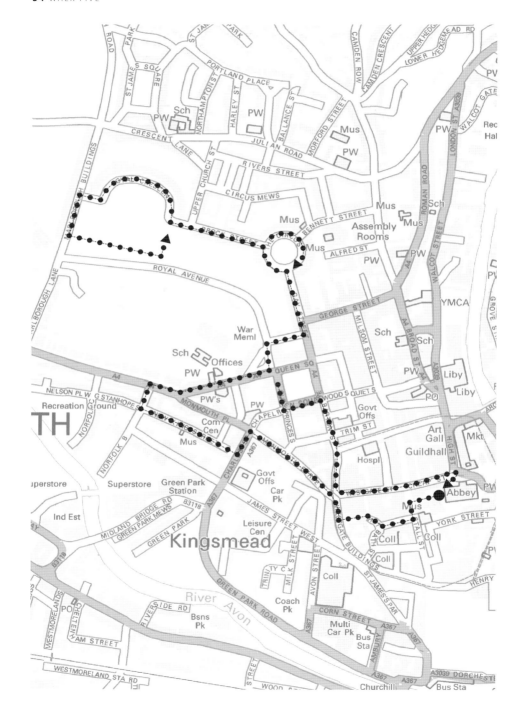

WALK 5
CIRCUS

Stand with your back to the Abbey door.
Make for the colonnade by the Roman
Baths. Go through the colonnade and turn
left then immediately right into Bath Street.
Look at Arlington House.

▶ *Who was the architect for Bath Street?*

Walk to the end of the street and on your left:

▶ *When is Thermae Bath Spa closed?*

3

Follow round to your left for a few metres
and then head straight up the alleyway
called Hetling Court. When you reach the
top, turn right into Westgate Buildings.
Look around you.

▶ *When was the Hospital of St John the
Baptist founded?*

4

Continue along the street and at the
junction pause in Kingsmead Square on
your left and study Rosewell House.

▶ *Who lived here?*

Retrace your steps and turn left into
Monmouth Street. On your right:

▶ *Whose Parish Hall?*

6

Continue along the street.

▶ *What is the name of the pub?*
▶ *Who insured number 27 against fire?*

At the end of the street turn left and then
right, down New King Street.

▶ *Where could you have hired a tandem?*
▶ *What is the date of this building?*

8

Continue down New King Street.

▶ *Who laid the foundation stone of the
original chapel?*
▶ *What happened in 1942?*

JOHN WESLEY IN BATH

You will have noticed that Wesley laid the foundation stone of the original Methodist chapel in New King Street. His connections with Bath were numerous – for example he founded Kingswood School in 1748 to educate the sons of Methodist preachers. Some continuity was needed as by definition Methodist preachers were itinerant.

Wesley came to the Bristol and Bath area at the invitation of George Whitefield who was himself returning to America to preach. He needed someone to take over in this area and John Wesley seemed the ideal person. The Bishop of Bristol at that time, Joseph Butler, was not entirely sure that he wanted Wesley preaching in his diocese because the style and content of Wesley's preaching was likely to overturn parish and diocesan discipline. The Bishop asked him to stop; Wesley of course could not.

In Bath Wesley's way of life and his preaching made a stark contrast to the lifestyle and values of Beau Nash. On one occasion when the two men met Nash accused Wesley of preaching sedition – stirring up revolution. According to Wesley's journal the argument was settled not by recourse to Bishops or the law but by an old woman: 'You, Mr Nash, take care of your body; we take care of our souls; and for the food of our souls we come here.' [To hear Mr Wesley preach.] Apparently Beau Nash had no reply to this and simply walked away.

Find number 19.

▶ *Who lived here in 1781?*

Turn right opposite number 31 and admire St Ann's Place then return to New King Street. Turn right at the end into Stanhope Place and continue up the hill towards the main road along Little Stanhope Street.

▶ *Which Saint has a house at number 5?*

Turn right and then cross carefully to Charlotte Street.

▶ *What has number 15 been in the past?*

Admire number 11 and when it is safe, cross the road and then look back across the road to the Elim Pentecostal Church.

▶ *What date can you find on this church?*

Cross the entrance to Charlotte Street car park and continue. You will arrive at Queen Square Place. At the corner of Queen Square turn left into Queen's Parade. Don't enter the park but turn right into Queen's Parade Place. Then turn left into Gay Street.

▶ *Who lived at number 8?*

At the top turn left into The Circus.

▶ *When was it erected?*
▶ *Who lived at number 7?*
▶ *Who lived at number 9?*

Turn left into Brock Street and walk along to number 7.

▶ *What can you find above the porch?*
▶ *What is odd about numbers 8 and 9?*

Continue along Brock Street and at the end cross to the cobbled beginning of Royal Crescent and look at number 1.

▶ *Who was generous?*

Walk along to number 5.

▶ *When did Christopher Anstey live here?*

Carry on along the Crescent to number 11.

▶ *What happened here on 18 March 1772?*

The Circus

Walk along to number 16.

▶ *What is number 16?*
▶ *Who lived at number 17?*

Pillars in the Circus: note the three different styles of capital topping the pillars

Continue to the end of the Crescent.

▶ *How long did it take for the Crescent to be built?*

Turn left and go down the hill. At the bottom of Marlborough Buildings, turn left along the path which crosses the park. Admire the Crescent from this path as you walk. At the junction of the paths turn left and walk up the path to Brock Street again. At the top cross and then turn right along Brock Street and you are on the opposite side to your earlier section. Immediately:

▶ *Who was Handel's right handel man?*

Cross Margaret's Buildings and continue along Brock Street. When you rejoin the Circus turn left and find house number 13.

▶ *Who lived here we presume?*

Continue on a little.

▶ *When did Lord Clive die?*

Now find house number 17.

▶ *Who lived here?*

A house on the Royal Crescent

 25

Cross Bennett Street and continue round the Circus.

▶ *How could you get an M.A. at number 22?*

 26

Turn left and walk down Gay Street on the right going down. At the bottom turn right into Queen Square. Walk along to number 24 and study the plaque on the railings.

▶ *When was Queen Square erected?*

 27

Continue along the pavement until the end of Queen Square then cross at the safety island. Walk down to number 16.

▶ *Whose residence was on this site?*

 28

At the bottom cross at the safety island again and continue round the square. At the canopy of the hotel carefully cross the road to the centre of the square.

▶ *When was Queen Square Lawn given to the city?*

 29

Walk up the path to the obelisk.

▶ *Who erected the obelisk?*

THEATRE ROYAL, OLD ORCHARD STREET

You could think of this as the 'old' Theatre Royal, the one that preceded the Theatre Royal in Saw Close. In its heyday this was the most important theatre outside London.

This is important for Bath as the city was becoming a major centre for leisure and for health. The theatre was built in 1750 by the architect and builder Thomas Jelly and it then received its Royal Licence in 1767. There is not much to see now either outside or in: it was gutted in 1809 when it became a Roman Catholic Chapel. It closed as a theatre in 1805.

Some important names were connected to its past: it was managed by the M.P. John Palmer (of mail coach fame) and the Royal Patent was the first ever granted to a theatre outside London. Famous names played at the Theatre Royal – Garrick, Kemble and Sarah Siddons who performed there from 1778–1782. Tradition has it that she then went off to haunt the Theatre Royal Bristol.

Retrace your steps and re-cross the road. Turn left and walk along to the junction and turn right down Barton Street. At the next junction turn right into Beauford Square. Study the large building on your left.

▶ *What decorates the roof line and the wall facing you?*

Return to Barton Street and turn right, walking down to Sawclose. As it becomes Sawclose study the information panel in the wall of the building on your right.

▶ *What colour does Juliana wear?*

Walk on to the Theatre Royal on your right.

▶ *When was the Theatre Royal built? This is in fact the 'New' Theatre Royal.*
▶ *Who was responsible for its building?*

Continue to the end of Sawclose and turn left into Westgate Street. Continue as it becomes Cheap Street and at the end you're back at the Abbey ●

Bishop Oliver King's rebus on the Abbey

REBUSES

My dictionary says that a rebus is 'a device suggesting the name of its bearer' if that's helpful! Easier, perhaps, is to say that it's a cross between a badge and a picture-puzzle which represents the person connected with the building concerned.

If you have binoculars (or particularly good eyesight!) you might just make out at the top of Rosewell House the shapes of a rose and a well, but don't feel defeated if you can't.

Far easier to spot (and much better known) is the rebus of Bishop Oliver King on the Abbey as you look at it from outside the entrance to the Roman Baths.

Oliver King was responsible for the building you see before you, and the story is that he had a dream in which he saw a host of angels on a ladder, and an olive tree with a crown on it. See if you can spot the olive (Oliver) and the crown (King).

Another famous rebus in the region is at the cathedral in Wells by Penniless Porch. See if you can spot a torch (beacon) and a barrel (tun). The bishop's name was Thomas Bekynton (beacon + tun). Clever!

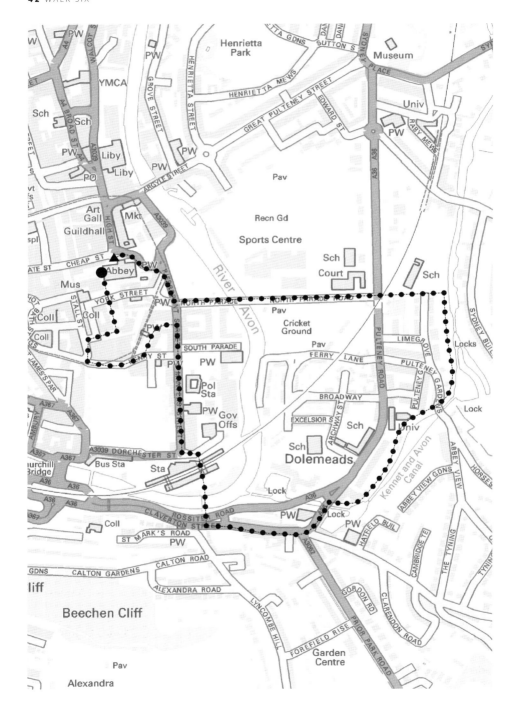

WALK 6
WIDCOMBE

With the main door of the Abbey behind you, turn to your left and make your way across the paved area. Leaving Tourist Information to your left, cross the road and enter Abbey Green. Go through the arch and take the road right into Abbey Gate Street. Turn left into Stall Street and left again at the end into New Orchard Street. Then turn left into Old Orchard Street.

▶ *What building do you find on your right?*
▶ *Study the plaque on this building: what was special about the Theatre Royal?*
▶ *What is the date on the building opposite ie. behind you!*
▶ *How much younger is the Manvers Gospel Hall?*

Move on round the corner and as you approach the pillars, find out:

▶ *Who lived at number 1?*

Walk up through the pillars and turn right into Pierrepont/ Manvers Street. Continue and cross the junction with Henry Street. Walk past the police station opposite and admire Manvers Street Baptist Church and the tower. When you are opposite the Baptist Church cross the road and continue down Manvers Street.

▶ *When was the Royal Hotel Bath established?*

Continue towards the station, admiring Brunel's design. Cross the road and walk though the tunnel on the pavement. When you are through the tunnel walk to the gatepost. This is made from two sections of Brunel's original broad-gauge rail. Cross the footbridge facing you.

▶ *Who was the engineer in 1877?*

Cross straight over at the lights. You are on a traffic island. Move to your left and cross the road to Claverton Buildings.

▶ *What number is Claverton House?*

Continue walking until you see Widcombe Parade opposite you.

▶ *Who has a court in Widcombe Parade?*
▶ *How many bells are there to be rung?*

Old Orchard Street, through North Parade Place

When you reach the pillar box look up.

▶ *What was provided at some time in the past?*

You have now moved to Sussex Place.

▶ *How would I get to Armes Court?*

9

Walk on to the bottom of Widcombe Hill.

▶ *What animal lives here?*

Very carefully cross the road and walk up Widcombe Hill until you reach the Church Room and Institute.

▶ *What is strange about the statue outside the Church Room and Institute?*
▶ *Who uses it now?*

HALFPENNY BRIDGE

The old bridge, which opened in 1863, was wooden. It had the toll house at the Widcombe end, charging people leaving (usually) the station.

In 1877 disaster struck. Scores of passengers coming from Weymouth to the showground of The Bath and West of England Agricultural Society waited patiently on the bridge to pay their toll to the one overworked and harassed collector. The bridge could not bear their weight and collapsed into the river. Some say eight people died, some 12, with upwards of 50 more injured.

The disaster was gruesome enough for *The London Illustrated News* to have a picture of the collapse in its copy of 18 June of that year.

Shortly afterwards a metal bridge was built as a replacement, which, we are confident, will take your weight!

11

Retrace your steps and carefully cross the road again and walk right, towards the chapel.

▶ *Who laid the two stones?*
▶ *What came up instead of the thorn?*

12

Taking great care, cross the road to the canal lock by St Matthew's Place.

▶ *Who made the paddle winding gear on the lock gate?*

13

Follow the tow path, watching out for the odd car. You are walking with the allotments on your right.

▶ *How many pairs of lock gates have you passed?*

14

Continue along the tow path and follow the slope up to the bridge.

▶ *What number is the bridge?*

15

Cross the road and continue on the tow path. You are now at lock 11.

▶ *Study the tower by the Pump Shed. Guess what it is.*

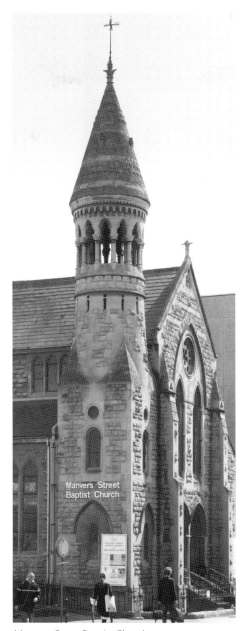

Manvers Street Baptist Church

In the car park behind Bath Spa station: a home-made gatepost, from pieces of Brunel's broad-gauge rail

Bridge with lock gate on the Widcombe flight

Keep walking past lock 12.

▶ *Who paid for the restoration of Widcombe Locks?*
▶ *How long did the restoration take?*

Continue walking to lock 13.

▶ *Who has a 'station' here?*

Carry on, walking past a flight of steps on your left, until you reach the Widcombe Lock Flight information board.

▶ *So, what was the tower/monument?*

Turn and look behind you.

▶ *Who owned the maltings? (This might be difficult when the leaves are out)*

Retrace your steps and descend the flight of steps, cross the end of the *cul de sac* and head for the arch. Go through the arch and turn left and cross at the lights under the bridge and walk down North Parade Road. On your right:

▶ *When are the courts open?*

The tower by the pump shed

Continue along the road until you are at the cricket ground.

▶ *What is the name of the building opposite?*

Continue along the road and cross the bridge by the sports centre. Study the plaque at the end of the bridge.

▶ *Who opened the bridge to traffic?*
▶ *When?*

Continue down North Parade. At the end, cross over and bear right. You are in the Orange Grove and back at the Abbey ●

WALK 7
PARADE GARDENS

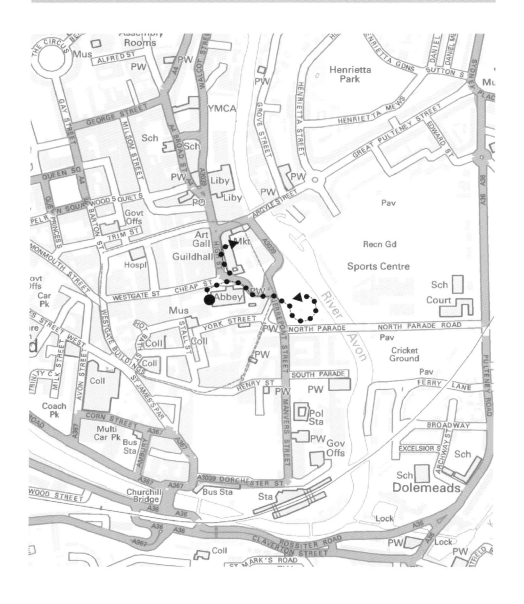

With the main Abbey door behind you, turn right and walk round to the fountain and cross the road at the lights. Turn right and follow the pavement for a few yards. Study the memorial stone on your left.

▶ *When was the Guildhall built?*

Carefully cross the road to the Obelisk.

▶ *When was Bath's friendship with Alkmaar cemented?*
▶ *Whose name can you find on the obelisk?*

The Astrolabe

Mozart being played – but in whose memory?

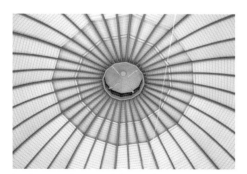

Looking up: the central dome of the market

Leave the garden and cross the road at the lights. Turn left and then enter Parade Gardens. In no particular order, how quickly can you find these?

▶ *In whose memory should Mozart be played?*
▶ *What words can you find under the Astrolabe?*
▶ *In which country is Kaposvar?*
▶ *Who planted the medlar?*
▶ *Who planted the other tree with a large plaque by it?*
▶ *How many sides has the bandstand?*
▶ *Who was the Peacemaker?*

Now leave the gardens by the same
way you entered. Turn right, following
the pavement along to the end. Cross left
at the lights. Walk back a few steps the way
you came (but now you are on the other
side of the road) and enter the market.

▶ *What are you NOT allowed to do with
vegetables in the market?*
▶ *When was the purpose-built indoor
market built?*

Find the Market Pillar.

▶ *What was the pillar or 'nail' used for?*

Find the central dome and look up.

▶ *How many window sections are there?*

Leave the indoor market by the main door
opposite the one you used to enter. Turn left
and you can see the Abbey again ●

QUIZ ANSWERS

WALK 1
ROUND THE ABBEY

1 Rector from 1991–92
2 A firemark Bath Sun Fire
3 A lovely pub
4 1634
5 Gallaway's Buildings
6 1818 ▶ Because Huguenots were being persecuted in France
7 It's another firemark: West of England, Exeter
8 The Dowager Lady Noble in 1962
9 Edgar was crowned the First King of All England
10 1760 ▶ MCLXXXIX
11 The North Gate or Northgate
12 Beau Nash House
13 14 'human' heads ▶ 1885
14 24
15 1987 ▶ King's and Queen's Bath
16 Area, Grandeur, Completeness
17 Seven arches appear to have been filled in

WALK 2
WALCOT

1 A sham castle
2 It was the corn market
3 Oddly, there are 11 windows
4 Everlasting ▶ You need to reflect
5 1736
6 Well, it's on St Michael's Church House, so it could be St Michael but the figure is clearly killing a dragon, so is it St George?
7 1903
8 Robert Southey
9 Environmental Award 1985
10 They were brewed in Reading, Bristol and Devonport. This is on a sign on the left-hand wall of the entrance to the 'garden'.
11 They don't match; it looks as if the right-hand one has had the top arch filled in
12 1842
13 It's turned into London Street
14 Cassandra ▶ 21 January 1805 ▶ Frances (Fanny) Burney in 1814
15 It was 'added to'
16 Ford Build(ings)
17 Sarah Siddons
18 They appear to be the markers of the Parish boundary St Walcot on the left and St Michael on the right
19 Ale House
20 Walcott Schools is carved in the stone under the pediment of the building in front of you
21 Founded 1763 ▶ Selina
22 From the faded painting on the right-hand wall you can see that it was a dairy
23 1552 ▶ Thomas Jelly
24 1713
25 The Bye and Cross Post ▶ The mail coach service throughout the country

WALK 3
PULTENEY

1 Ralph Allen lived next door to the Friends Meeting House
2 1766
3 1694 ▶ Admiral Lord Nelson
4 William Wordsworth
5 Oliver Goldsmith ▶ The Chapel of St John of Beverley for the deaf and dumb
6 David Aust ▶ 1836
7 Two – the towers of the Abbey are not spires!
8 15 December 1727 ▶ Bath Rugby
9 2 June 1972
10 Bladud
11 That the building had been a lending library – and see also the lettering above the picture
12 William Pitt. It does not tell you on the plaque but he was Pitt the Younger.
13 Hannah More ▶ A sedan chair
14 Napoleon 3rd
15 Fred Weatherly K.C. He wrote the song 'Danny Boy'. The story is that he had this mock Tudor window made to stop people looking in at him so easily!
16 16
17 The Pulteney Arms ▶ 1759
18 Captain F.W. Forester
19 King George V
20 In the stone is carved 'Laura Chapel' ▶ It also appears above 25 and 26
21 You may not deposit rubbish or cause a nuisance – or drive a lorry over 3T
22 Six ▶ Thomas Baldwin and others
23 A lion and a unicorn, in the coat of arms of Queen Charlotte, wife of King George III
24 Robert Adam ▶ 1769–74
25 Since 1284

WALK 4
ASSEMBLY ROOMS

1 St Andrew
2 Sir Thomas Lawrence, president of the Royal Academy
3 Circular pattern in the wood
4 Rounded arch doorway ▶ Crenellations, like a castle
5 Montpellier
6 1798 ▶ 1856
7 A bay window
8 It looks like a long cone mounted on a bracket. It is a torch snuffer from the days of night-time transport in sedan chairs ▶ They are, or appear to have been, blocked in ▶ George
9 1771 ▶ John Wood the Younger ▶ In the card room
10 King Alfred ▶ It has a hoist
11 A canopied balcony ▶ The Porter ▶ £2 – but do not try it!
12 12
13 The Jane Austen Centre ▶ A carving of a face
14 Blue – they are probably Delft tiles
15 1781
16 Cheesemongers
17 A firemark saying 'Guardian' from the days when insurance companies ran the fire service and would only put out the fires of paid-up customers!
18 General Wolfe
19 It is part of the medieval city wall
20 1738
21 Union Passage

WALK 5
CIRCUS

1 Thomas Baldwin
2 Christmas Day, Boxing Day and New Year's Day
3 1174
4 Bishop Butler
5 St Paul's
6 The Griffin ▶ Bath Sun Fire
7 At number 56 ▶ in the past ▶ 1880
8 John Wesley in 1777 ▶ The second Methodist Chapel was destroyed in an air raid
9 William Herschel
10 St Agnes
11 A rectory
12 MDCCCLIV
13 Mrs Piozzi
14 1754–69 ▶ The Earl of Chatham ▶ Lord Leighton, President of the Royal Academy
15 A fire mark for Bath Sun Fire ▶ They have a large tower porch, unlike the others
16 Bernard Gilbert Stancomb Cayzer
17 1770–1805
18 Elizabeth Linley eloped from here with Richard Brinsley Sheridan
19 The Royal Crescent Hotel ▶ Sir Isaac Pitman, creator of Pitman's shorthand
20 1767–1775 ▶ Eight years
21 John Christopher Smith
22 David Livingstone, famous explorer
23 He died in 1774
24 Thomas Gainsborough
25 Major Andre lived here ▶ An M and an A
26 1728–35
27 William Oliver M.D.
28 1948
29 Richard Nash
30 Four lyres on the roof and six masks on the wall, five garlands and a crest
31 Grey
32 1805 ▶ George Dance the Younger and John Palmer

WALK 6
WIDCOMBE

1 The Masonic Hall ▶ It was the holder of the first Royal Patent ever granted to a provincial theatre ▶ 1852 ▶ 102 years younger
2 Elizabeth Anne Linley who later became Mrs R.B. Sheridan
3 1846
4 T.E.M. Marsh
5 17a
6 Bartlett ▶ Five bells
7 Surgical appliances, amongst other things
8 I would walk up Millbrook Place
9 A white hart
10 It has a bucket of flowers for a head ▶ The Natural Theatre Company
11 F.W. Spear laid one and the other was laid by Sir G.W. MacAlpine ▶ The fir tree came up instead of the thorn
12 Llewellin Gears Bristol
13 You have passed six pairs
14 196
15 Well done for guessing – the answer comes later!
16 The City of Bath and the Kennet and Avon Canal Trust ▶ Seven years: 1969–1976
17 Bath Humane Society
18 It was actually a chimney for the pumping station
19 Hugh Baird and Sons
20 9.00–4.30 Monday to Friday
21 The Pavilion
22 His Worship the Mayor W.F. Long ▶ July 1937

WALK 7
PARADE GARDENS

1 MDCCLXXVII
2 5 May 1945 ▶ Richard Nash
3 Mark Purnell 1938–1985 ▶ Nisi serenas horas non numero ▶ Hungary ▶ The Royal Commonwealth Society planted the medlar ▶ Councillor Mrs Jan Hole ▶ The bandstand has six sides ▶ King Edward VII
4 You are not allowed to throw vegetables in the market ▶ 1861
5 For completing transactions/paying
6 There are 12 window sections

SCRAMBLED BATH ANSWERS

1. Pulteney Bridge | 2. Royal Crescent | 3. The Pump Rooms | 4. Sham Castle
5. North Parade | . Milsom Street | 7. Assembly Rooms | 8. Orange Grove
9. Beau Nash | 10. Thomas Baldwin | 11. Robert Nash | 12. Ralph Allen
13. Juliana Popjoy | 14. Doctor Oliver | 15. Sedan Chair | 16. Sul-Minerva